# CURIOUS FESTIVALS FROM AROUND THE WORLD

## Geography for Kids
## Children's Geography & Culture Books

Everyone loves a festival, right? In this book, we will be exploring some extreme festivals throughout the world. While you might enjoy some of them, there are some that might just be too extreme!

# MONKEY BUFFET FESTIVAL (THAILAND)

It's not what you think! The Monkey Buffet Festival, which is held each year in Lopburi, Thailand, involves serving a buffet meal to about 3,000 monkeys. The feast includes about 9,000 pounds of cakes, vegetables, and fruits that are laid out elegantly on tables and picnic blankets.

# LA TOMATINA
# (SPAIN)

Known to perhaps be the biggest food fight around the world, La Tomatina is a festival that takes place in Bunol, Valencia on the last Wednesday of August each year. Approximately 150,000 tomatoes are flung each year at its participants.

The fight typically will last about an hour, and the town square will be covered with debris from the tomatoes. The streets are then hosed down by the fire trucks and people will often use hoses provided by the locals to remove the debris from their bodies. Some of the participants will head to the "los peñones" pool to wash off.

La Tomatina

# WIFE-CARRYING WORLD CHAMPIONSHIP (FINLAND)

Each year, men gather in Sonkajärvi, Finland to compete in one of the most curious sporting events around, known as the Wife-Carrying World Championship. Men have to carry a wife (although it's not necessary that it's their wife) throughout an obstacle course. They can carry the wife piggyback, over the shoulder, or hang the wife upside-down with her legs hanging around the man's shoulders. The winner of this competition is paid the wife's weight in beer.

# NAKI SUMO
# (TOKYO)

While no mother likes to hear her baby cry, at the Naki Sumo baby crying contest, it is encouraged.

Sensoji Temple

This contest is held at the Sensoji Temple, located in Tokyo, each year and the festival has been a tradition for 400 years. The participants believe that it keeps the toddlers in good health as well as warding off evil spirits. The babies are held high towards the sky by sumo wrestlers who try to make them cry, with a sumo referee as a judge. The child who cries the loudest and the longest is named as the winner.

# MOOSE DROPPING FESTIVAL (ALASKA)

The Moose Dropping Festival which took place in Talkeetna, Alaska for 37 years, was pretty much what you think it might be. The festival centered around a raffle and numbered moose droppings were dropped onto a target from a net bag. Also involved was a betting game that involved tossing moose "nuggets" that had been painted, onto a board. Also included during this festival was the "Mountain Mother" contest, which involved a game of strength for local married women.

Talkeetna, Alaska
NAGLEY'S STORE
TALKEETNA ALASKA
WEST RIB
DELI & PUB
TALKEETNA
DENALI
VISITOR CENTER
LIQUOR STORE
KALADI
BROTHERS
COFFEE
OPEN
ICE
ROOT
BEER

Talkeetna, Alaska

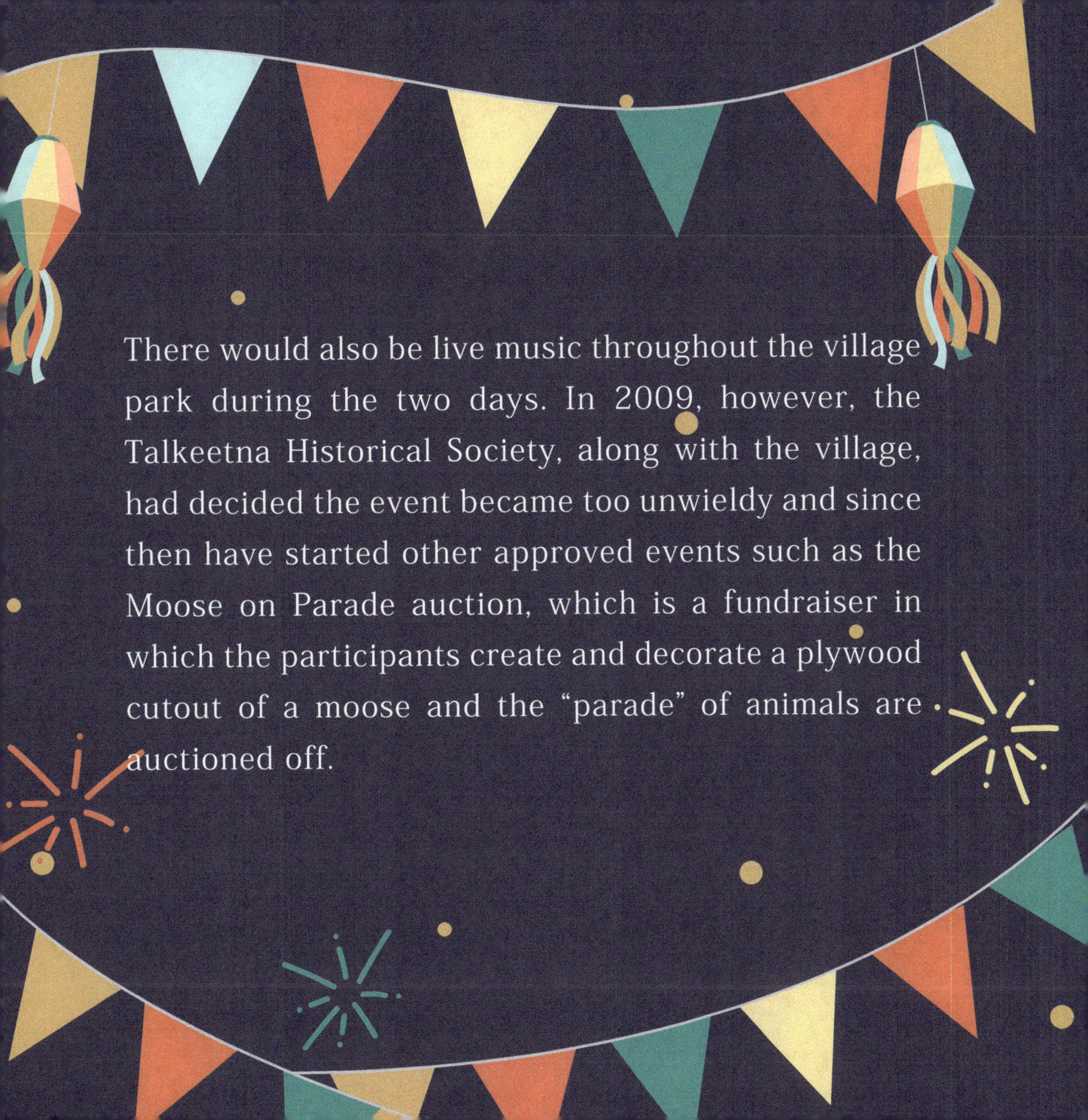

There would also be live music throughout the village park during the two days. In 2009, however, the Talkeetna Historical Society, along with the village, had decided the event became too unwieldy and since then have started other approved events such as the Moose on Parade auction, which is a fundraiser in which the participants create and decorate a plywood cutout of a moose and the "parade" of animals are auctioned off.

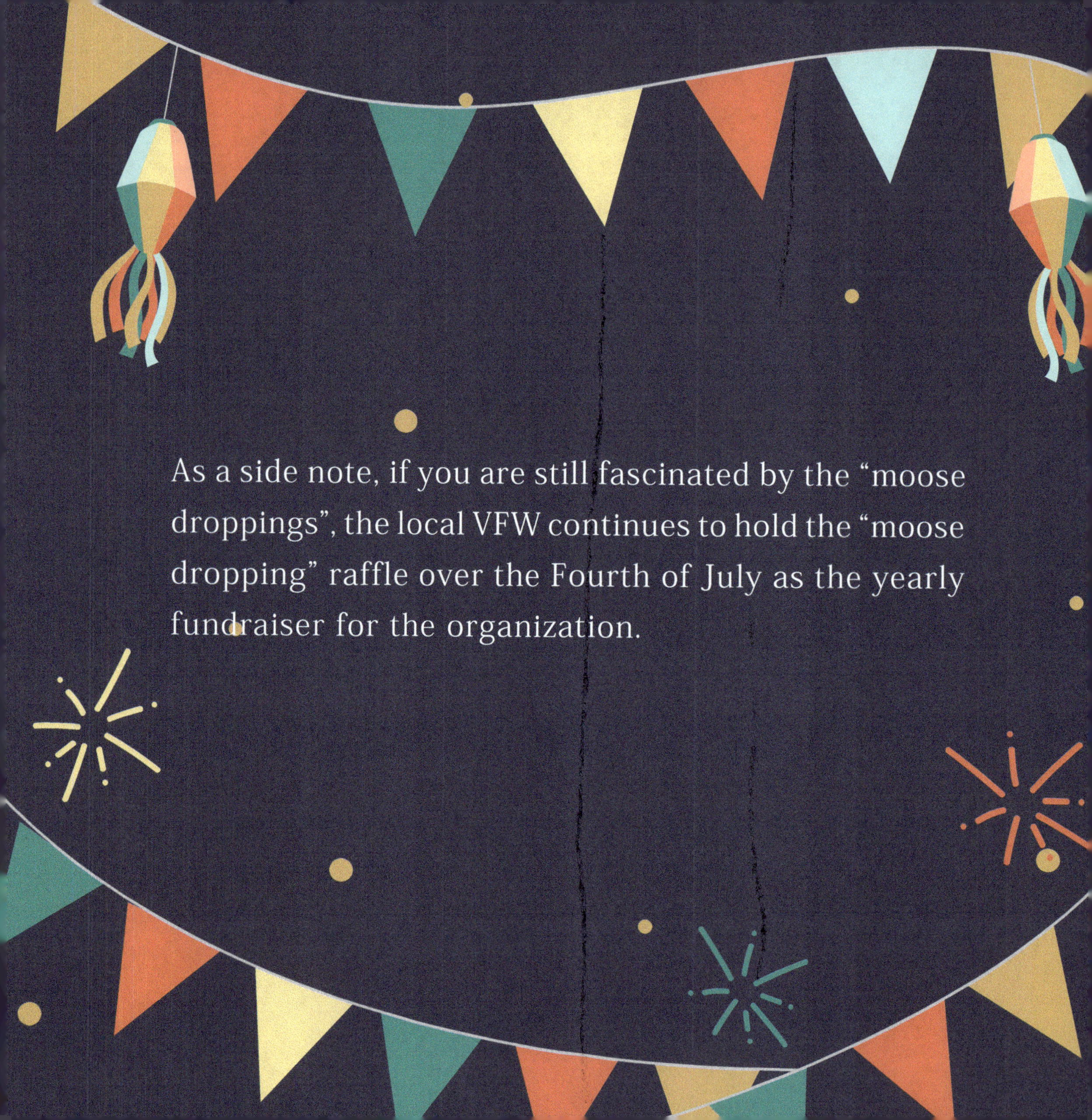

As a side note, if you are still fascinated by the "moose droppings", the local VFW continues to hold the "moose dropping" raffle over the Fourth of July as the yearly fundraiser for the organization.

WELCOME
TO BEAUTIFUL
DOWNTOWN
TALKEETNA

World Bog Snorkelling Location

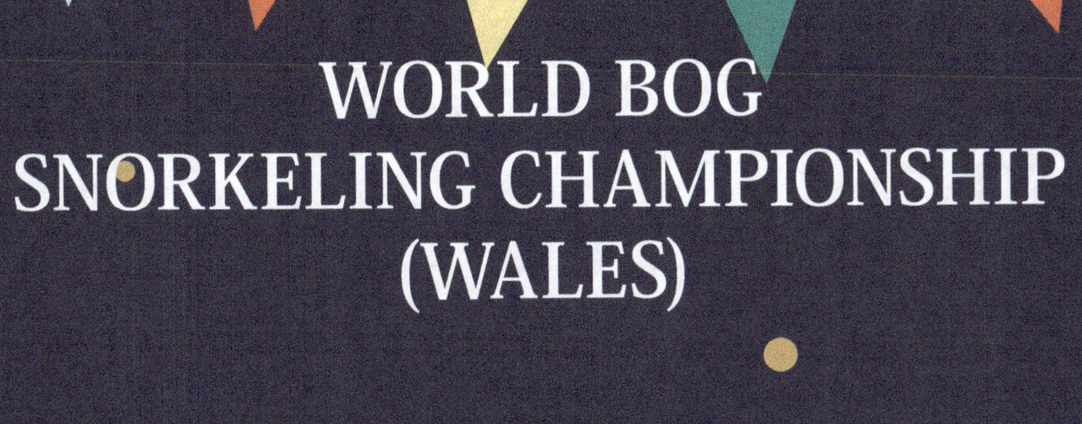

# WORLD BOG SNORKELING CHAMPIONSHIP (WALES)

While you may have tried snorkeling near a coral reef, the World Bog Snorkeling Championship is not what you might think. The championship is held in Wales at the Waen Rhydd peat bog located near Llanwrtyd Wells. The contest involves the competitors racing through a trench cut through a peat bog. The participant can use their snorkel gear; however, they are not going to have any beautiful views in this murky water.

In case you are wondering, peat forms as the material from plants does not decay fully in anaerobic and acidic conditions and is comprised mostly of wetland vegetation; primarily bog plants including sedges, mosses, and shrubs.

Worm Charming

# INTERNATIONAL FESTIVAL OF WORM CHARMING (ENGLAND)

Taking place in Blackawton, England, the International Festival of Worm Charming occurs each year in May. This sport involves the participants doing whatever they can to get the worms to come out from the ground. Forking and digging are not permitted.

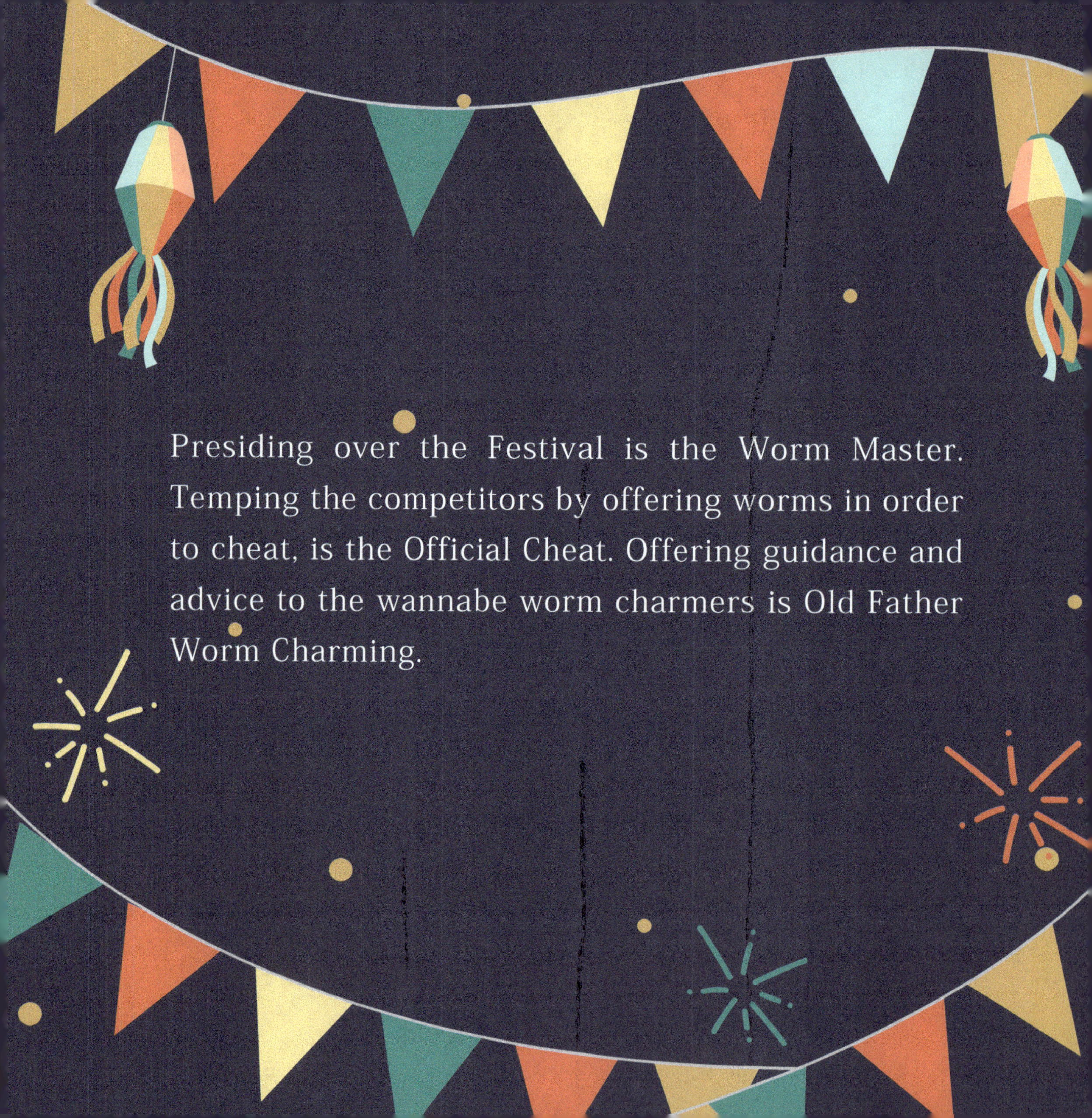

Presiding over the Festival is the Worm Master. Temping the competitors by offering worms in order to cheat, is the Official Cheat. Offering guidance and advice to the wannabe worm charmers is Old Father Worm Charming.

Blackawton, England

CENTENARY OF
BLACKAWTON
PARISH COUNCIL 1894 1994
CHURCH HILL

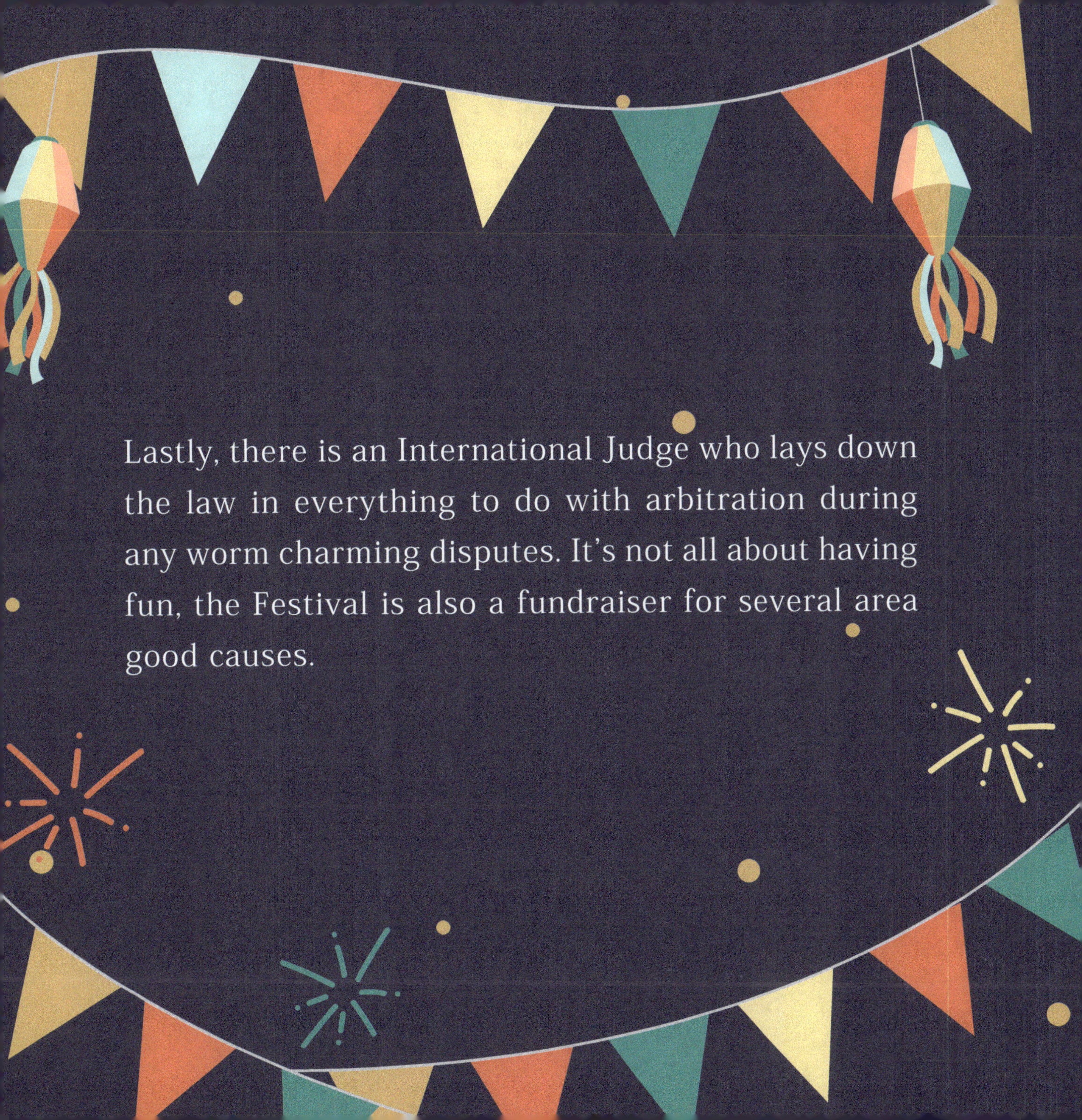

Lastly, there is an International Judge who lays down the law in everything to do with arbitration during any worm charming disputes. It's not all about having fun, the Festival is also a fundraiser for several area good causes.

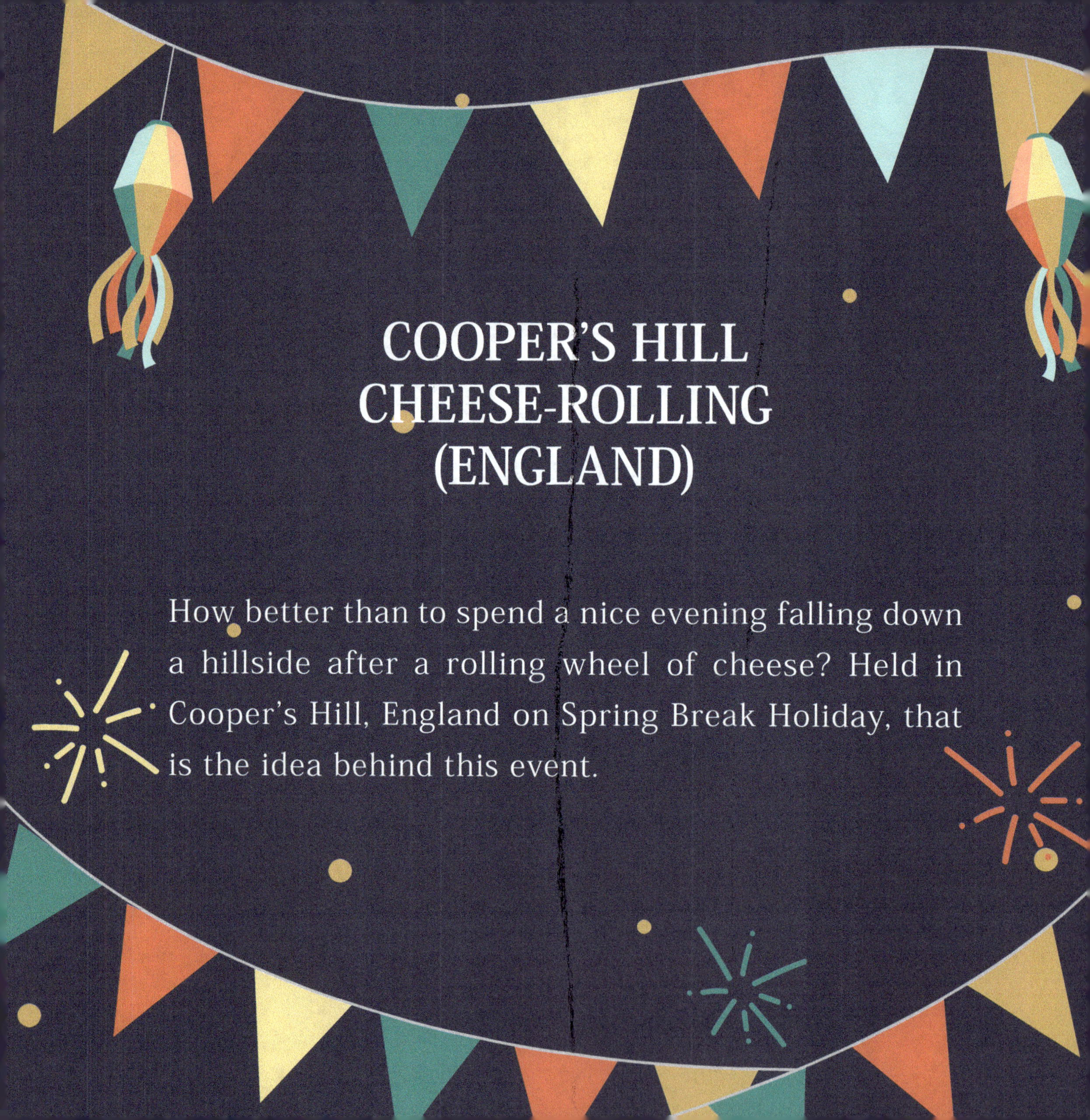

# COOPER'S HILL
# CHEESE-ROLLING
# (ENGLAND)

How better than to spend a nice evening falling down a hillside after a rolling wheel of cheese? Held in Cooper's Hill, England on Spring Break Holiday, that is the idea behind this event.

Cheese Rolling

The competition is a race to see who can arrive at the bottom of the hill before anyone else. While highly unlikely, the participants are supposed to catch the cheese as it rolls at a speed up to 70 mph.

# BUSÓJÁRÁS
# (HUNGARY)

This festival takes place in the town of Mohács. This festival is held over six days at the end of February and is intended to scare winter away. It is named for the busós, people that dress up in frightening and ornate costumes including big wooly cloaks and wooden masks.

DA POKLADESU

Over 500 busós arrive for the festival in rowboats traveling over the Danube River to take their place in the parade and participate in the other festivities. The idea is to scare winter away and welcome spring.

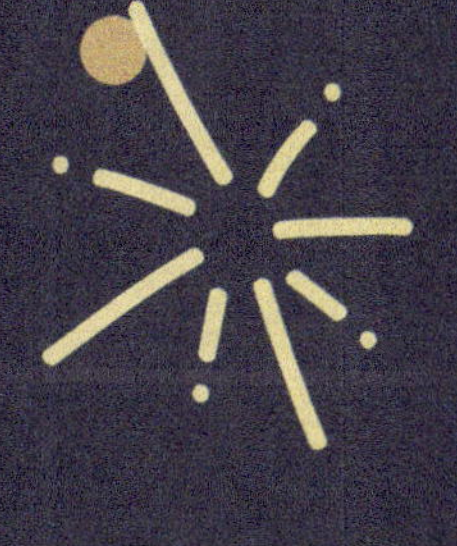

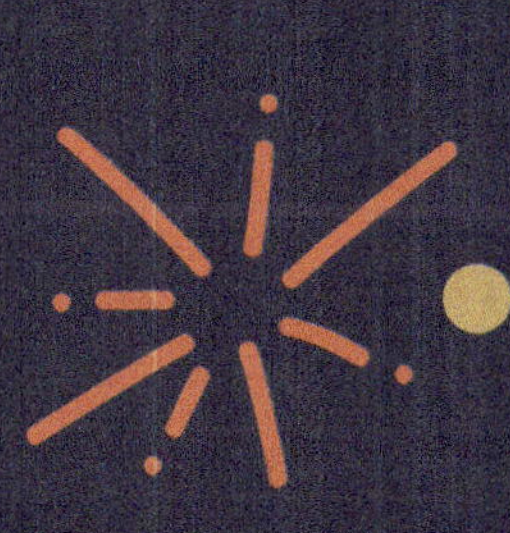

# THE INTERNATIONAL HIGHLINE MEETING FESTIVAL, MONTE PIANA (ITALY)

If you want to "chill out", you might be interested in the International Highline Meeting festival. However, it might be terrifying – attendees spend time stretched across tightropes along the Italian Alps located in Monte Piana, Italy, along the Italian Alps.

Monte Piana

Highline Meeting

Participants refer to themselves as "slackers" since they balance themselves on slacklines. This sport is different that tightrope walking since the rope is slightly flattened and has slack which means that it can bounce or move from side-to-side.

Along with the slackers spending most of their days and nights on these slacklines that are suspended hundreds of feet above the Alps, you will also find everything typical of a festival; a bar, a kitchen, and great musical jam sessions. You can also take tandem paraglider flights or attend a yoga workshop.

Monte Piana

Yorkshire Puddings

# YORKSHIRE PUDDING BOAT RACE

The vessels for this race are baked using Yorkshire's special recipe that involves eggs, water, and flour. Participants jump into their "canoes" (which are surprisingly stable) and paddle them down the river. Would you trust a canoe make from eggs, flour, and water? The canoes are coated with varnish as additional protection to keep them from sinking.

Originally, these vessels were used as rescue boats during time of flooding, but has since turned into part of English Folklore. While it may seem difficult to believe that these boats can hold water, the yacht

varnish is the special ingredient that makes the vessels able to race in Bob's Pond without sinking. Bob's Pond is in a small village known as Brawby, located North Yorkshire, England.

El Colacho

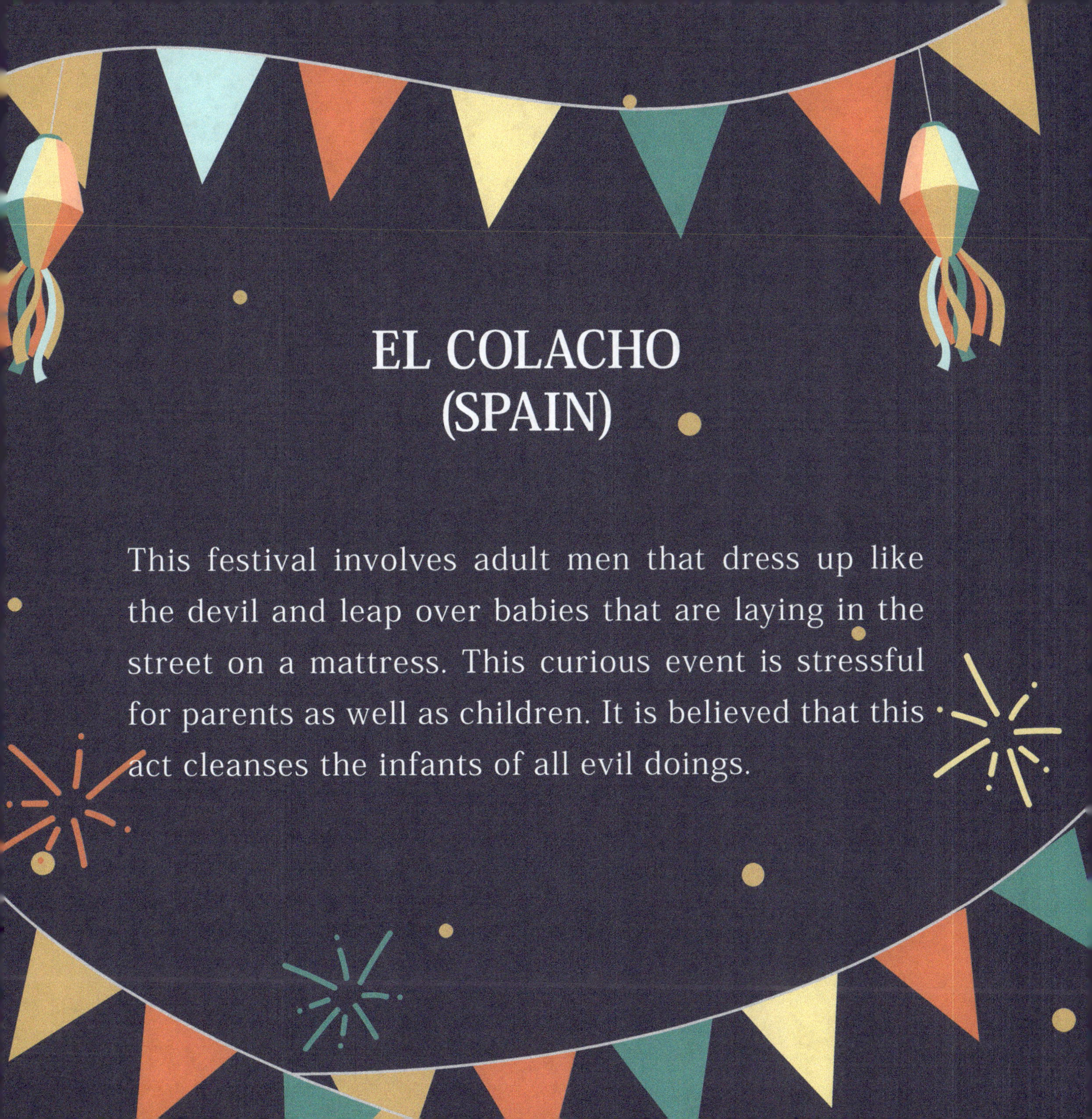

# EL COLACHO
# (SPAIN)

This festival involves adult men that dress up like the devil and leap over babies that are laying in the street on a mattress. This curious event is stressful for parents as well as children. It is believed that this act cleanses the infants of all evil doings.

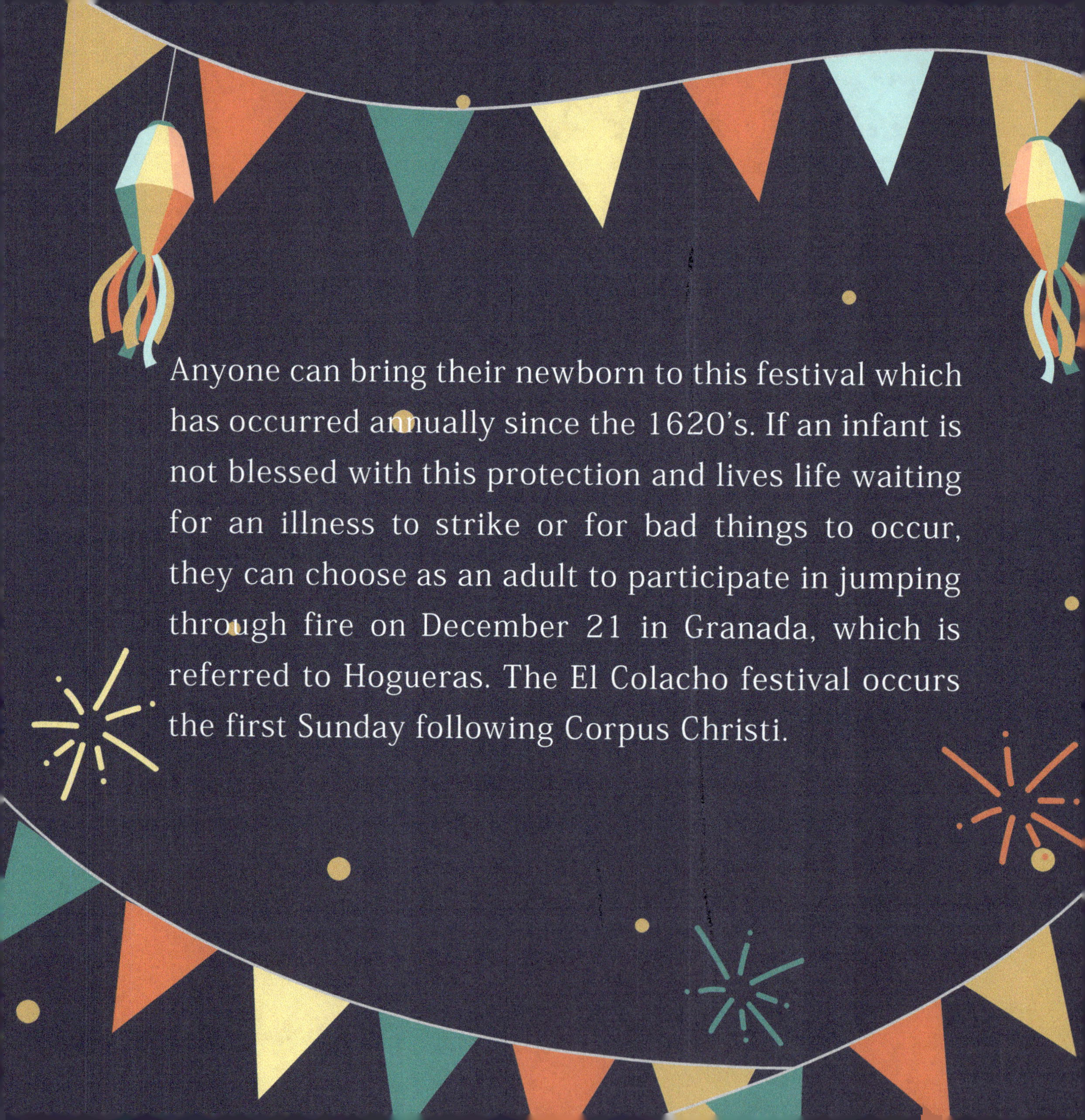

Anyone can bring their newborn to this festival which has occurred annually since the 1620's. If an infant is not blessed with this protection and lives life waiting for an illness to strike or for bad things to occur, they can choose as an adult to participate in jumping through fire on December 21 in Granada, which is referred to Hogueras. The El Colacho festival occurs the first Sunday following Corpus Christi.

El Colacho

# HOLI FESTIVAL OF COLORS

The Holi Festival welcomes spring's arrival and winter's passing. There is an atmosphere of social merriment as people bury their hatchets and toss their worries to the wind. Color is everywhere and both adults and youngsters are covered in colors, including green, red, blue, yellow, orange, pink, and violet, to name a few. Small groups of people dance, sing, and throw colors on one another.

# GOLDEN RETRIEVER FESTIVAL (SCOTLAND)

If you like dogs, you will enjoy this festival! The Golden Retriever Club of Scotland holds this festival at the breeds' ancestral home. Commemorating the club's 50th anniversary in 2006, the first festival took place with 188 goldens participating.

At that time, it was the largest group to be photographed in one place. The most recent record in 222 dogs.

Have you decided on a festival you would like to attend? If not, there are many more curious festivals that take place around the world. For additional information, you can visit your local library, research the internet, and ask questions of your teachers, family and friends.

Visit

**BABY PROFESSOR**
EDUCATION KIDS

# www.BabyProfessorBooks.com

to download Free Baby Professor eBooks
and view our catalog of new and exciting
Children's Books